Some Kids Are Deaf

Revised and Updated

by Lola M. Schaefer

Consulting Editor: Gail Saunders-Smith, PhD
Consultant: Judith M. Gilliam
Former Board Member
National Association for the Deaf

Pebble Books are published by Capstone Press,
1710 Roe Crest Drive, North Mankato, Minnesota 56003.
www.capstonepub.com

 Books published by Capstone Press are manufactured with paper
containing at least 10 percent post-consumer waste.

Library of Congress Cataloging-in-Publication Data
Schaefer, Lola M., 1950–
    Some kids are deaf / by Lola M. Schaefer. — Rev. and updated.
    p. cm.—(Pebble books. Understanding differences)
    Includes bibliographical references and index.
    ISBN-13: 978-1-4296-0811-4 (hardcover)   ISBN-13: 978-1-4296-1775-8 (softcover pbk.)
    ISBN-10: 1-4296-0811-0 (hardcover)   ISBN-10: 1-4296-1775-6 (softcover pbk.)
    1. Deaf children—Juvenile literature. 2. Deafness—Juvenile literature. I. Title.
II. Series.
HV2392.S33 2008
362.4'2—dc22   2007009114

Summary: Simple text and photographs describe kids who are deaf, the ways they
communicate, and some of their everyday activities.

Note to Parents and Teachers

The Understanding Differences set supports national social studies
standards related to individual development and identity. This book
describes children who are deaf and illustrates their special needs.
The photographs support early readers in understanding the text. The
repetition of words and phrases helps early readers learn new words.
This book also introduces early readers to subject-specific vocabulary
words, which are defined in the Glossary. Early readers may need
assistance to read some words and to use the Table of Contents,
Glossary, Read More, Internet Sites, and Index sections
of the book.

Printed in the United States of America in North Mankato, Minnesota.
042014   008121R

Table of Contents

Deafness

Some kids are deaf.
Kids who are deaf
cannot hear.

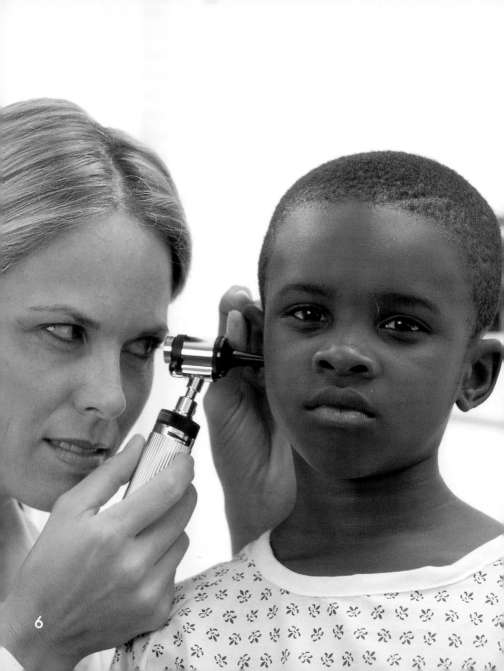

Some kids are born deaf.
Other kids become deaf
from a sickness or from
getting hurt.

Tools for Hearing

Some kids can hear a little.
They wear hearing aids
to hear sounds louder.

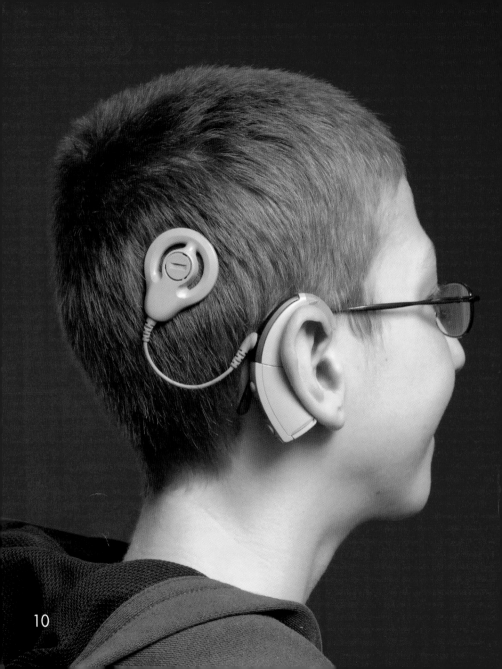

Some kids who are deaf get cochlear implants. Implants help them hear some sounds.

BRAIN TEASER!
Level A
Morgan
Melissa
Aisha
Cullen
Taylor
dirty
frown
play
found
take
28

Talking

Some kids who are deaf use sign language to talk. Sign language is hand signs that stand for letters, words, and numbers.

Sign Language

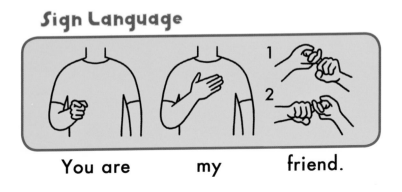

You are   my   friend.

Some kids who are deaf use their voice to talk. Speech therapists teach them to speak clearly.

Everyday Life

Kids who are deaf depend on their sense of sight. Flashing lights tell them it's time for class.

TV G

MACAPA●

AMAZON BASIN

BRAZIL

STRADDLING THE EQUATOR, MACAPA, BRAZIL IS AN EXOTIC WORLD

ORION

MTS STEREO

Kids who are deaf watch TV with closed captioning. The words tell what people on TV are saying.

Kids who are deaf depend on their sense of touch. They can feel a pager vibrate when a friend sends a text message.

Glossary

cochlear implant—a small electronic device that is surgically put into a person's head; cochlear implants allow sounds to get to the brain.

deaf—being unable to hear

hearing aid—a small electronic device that people wear in or behind one or both ears; hearing aids make sounds louder.

pager—a small electronic device that can receive and send text messages

senses—ways of learning about your surroundings; hearing, smelling, touching, tasting, and sight are the five senses.

sign language—hand signs that stand for words, letters, and numbers

speech therapist—a person who is trained to help people learn to speak clearly

text message—words sent from a pager or cell phone to another person's pager or cell phone

Read More

Kelley, Walter P. *Deaf Culture A to Z.* Austin, Texas: Buto Limited, 2003.

Petelinsek, Kathleen, and E. Russell Primm. *At School/ En la escuela.* Talking Hands. Chanhassen, Minn.: Child's World, 2006.

Royston, Angela. *Deafness.* What's It Like? Chicago: Heinemann Library, 2005.

Internet Sites

FactHound offers a safe, fun way to find Internet sites related to this book. All of the sites on FactHound have been researched by our staff.

Here's how:

1. Visit *www.facthound.com*

2. Choose your grade level.

3. Type in this book ID **1429608110** for age-appropriate sites. You may also browse subjects by clicking on letters, or by clicking on pictures and words.

4. Click on the **Fetch It** button.

FactHound will fetch the best sites for you!

Index

Word Count: 152
Early-Intervention Level: 14

Editorial Credits
Rebecca Glaser, revised edition editor; Mari C. Schuh, editor; Bob Lentz, revised
edition designer; Kelly Garvin, photo stylist; Katy Kudela, photo researcher

Photo Credits
Arthur Tilley/FPG International LLC, 6
Capstone Press/Karon Dubke, cover, 4, 8, 10, 12, 14, 16, 18, 20

Acknowledgments
Pebble Books thanks the staff and students of the Minnesota State Academy for
the Deaf in Faribault, Minnesota, especially Roxanne Mitchell and Adrian Hagen, for
their assistance with the photographs in this book.